Nature Mazes

Suzanne Ross

DOVER PUBLICATIONS, INC.
New York

Bibliographical Note

Nature Mazes is a new work, first published by Dover Publications, Inc., in 1994.

Note

Each of the 44 mazes in this book concerns some aspect of the natural world. As you enjoy working these mazes, see what you learn about different creatures and habitats, and make sure to follow the directions for those mazes with special rules. The solutions are given at the back of the book, beginning on page 49.

Help this hungry spider go to the middle of his web. There he can feel the vibrations to find his trapped insect dinner.

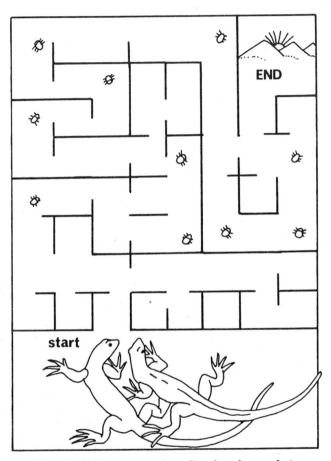

The lizards must gather five beetles *each* (a total of ten) before they take a nap in the sunny desert.

Help the African bush baby to join its friend high in the rain-forest canopy. It is dark and time for it to hunt insects with its big eyes and ears.

6

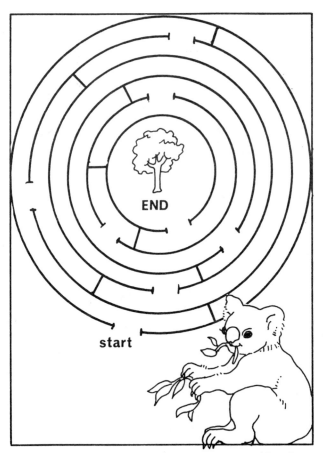

START

END

This baby koala is big enough to stay outside of mom's pouch, where he has been growing. Help him find his home in the eucalyptus tree.

7

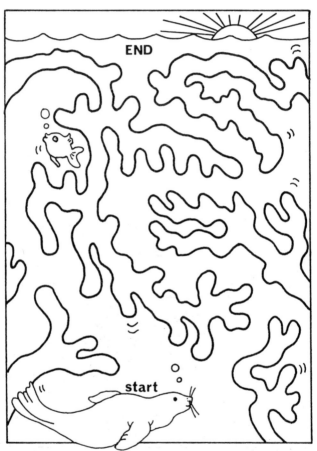

Find the correct path for this seal. He needs to swim to the surface for a breath of fresh air and a peek at the sunset.

8

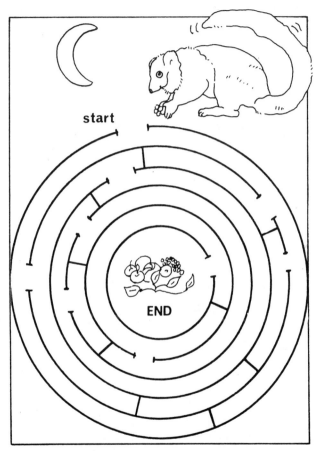

start

END

It is nighttime in the treetops, time to search for seeds, flowers, fruit and leaves, a lemur's favorite food. Find the correct path.

9

END

start

This bighorn sheep lives in the Rocky Mountains in the U.S.A. Help it reach a juicy favorite plant high on the mountaintop.

END

start

The Amazon River winds across the widest part of South America. Find the path the river takes to flow into the ocean.

11

Mamma stork wants to return to her nest and baby storks. Help her find a path around the clouds.

12

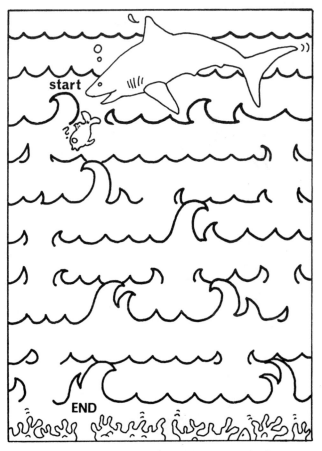

start

END

Which path will the salmon take to hide from the shark among the sea plants?

start

END

The rain-forest orchid is sending out a scent that attracts bees. Help this bee find the correct path so it can do its job of pollination.

14

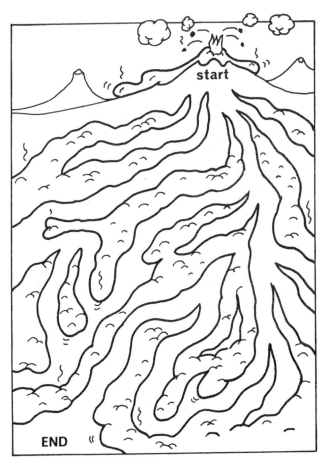

start

END

Smoke, fire, flying coals and hot lava are given off by an erupting volcano. Find an escape path through the hot flowing lava to safety.

start

END

Find the correct path through the rain forest
from friend to friend so these chimpanzees can
play together.

16

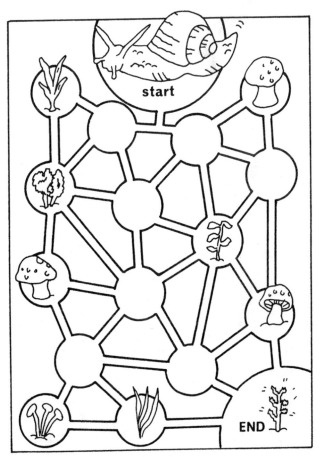

start

END

Make a slimy trail while gathering six tasty plants from start to end, but don't touch the poison mushrooms!

17

start

END

It's winter! Help this hummingbird fly from your house to the rain forest, where it is moist and warm.

Help this African elephant reach the forest. She is the biggest land animal and needs to eat lots of grasses, twigs and bark.

19

Help this tiger follow the correct path to the forest, where he can hunt and eat prey.

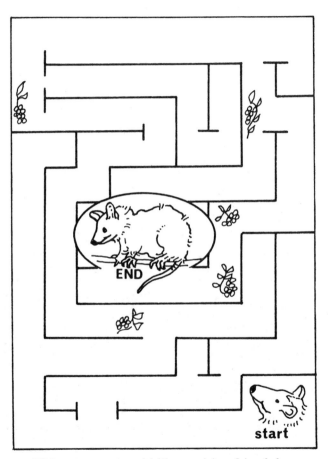

This opossum would like to visit a friend, but
must gather five bunches of berries on the way.

21

This crab has spotted a hungry sea otter and
must find a path to the rocks, where it can hide.

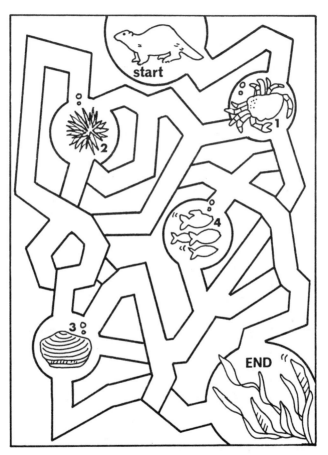

Help the sea otter gather all four of its favorite foods: crab, sea urchin, shellfish and fish. Then it can sleep in its seaweed bed.

23

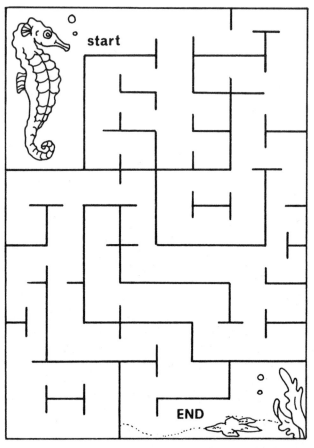

start

END

Help this sea horse swim to the bottom of the
sea, where it can curl its tail around a sea plant.

24

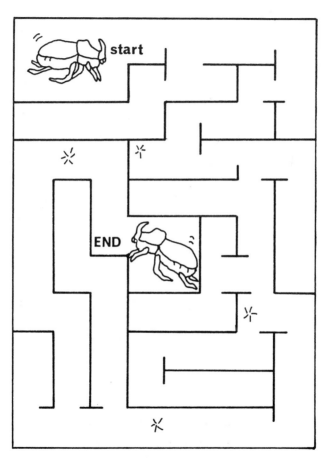

start

END

This rhinoceros beetle senses a foe in its territory. Help it find the intruder, which it must battle and chase away.

25

start

END

This rhinoceros wants to travel to a muddy
pool of water, where it can roll around and cool
26   off. Help it find its way.

start

END

Two baby sea turtles have broken out of their eggs deep in the sand. Can you help them reach the ocean?

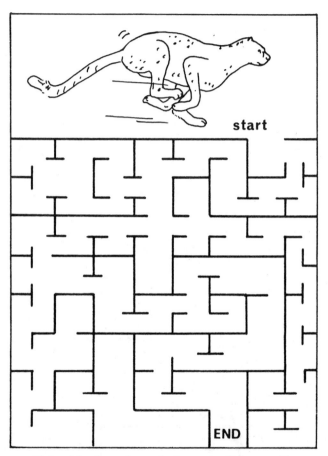

start

END

Help this cheetah reach the end of his run. He can move at speeds of up to 60 miles per hour, so your trip should be quick!

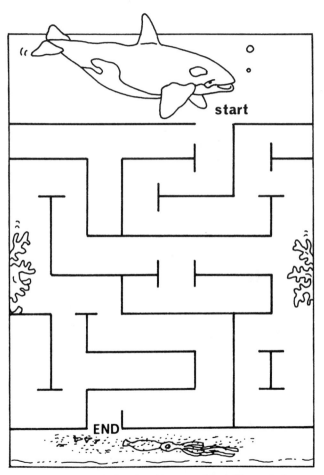

start

END

To get squid for its dinner, this killer whale
must find a path to the ocean bottom. 29

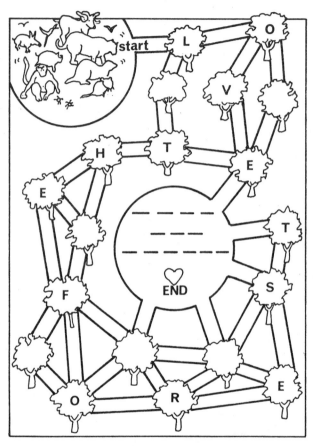

What are the rain-forest animals trying to tell us? Each blank in the circle needs a letter from the tree path. As you follow the path fill in each letter (do not pass through empty trees).

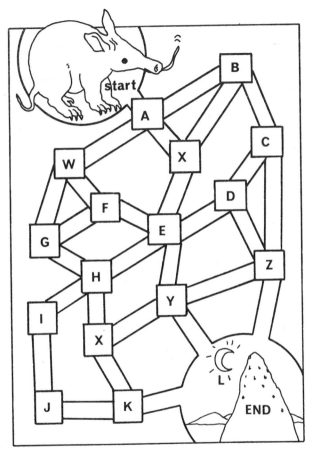

This aardvark wants to find a big termite mound so it can dine by the light of the moon. Follow the letters in alphabetical order from A (for aardvark) to L (for light).

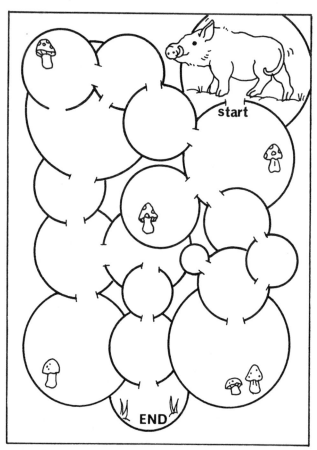

Help this wild pig find a watery place, where he can root around for plants and insects (but he must avoid the poisonous mushrooms along the path).

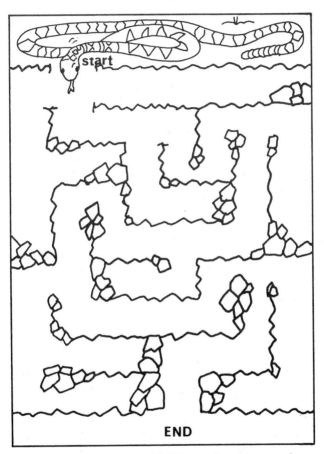

start

END

This rattlesnake would like to sleep in a cool
dark place. Help it find a path to the bottom of
this lonesome old mine in the desert.   33

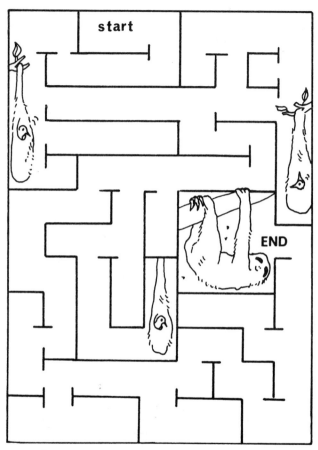

start

END

Follow the path that leads to the sloth who is pretending to be a bird's nest in the rain forest. He is the one with moths living in his greenish hair!

34

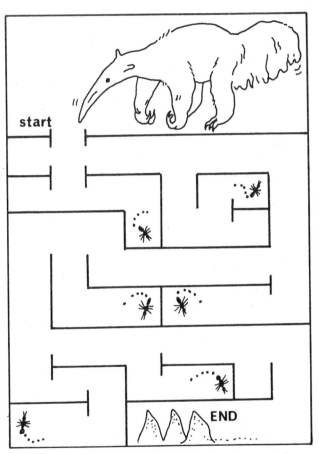

start

END

Help this giant anteater leave the direct path
six times to gather stray ants on his way to their
big anthill in time for dinner.

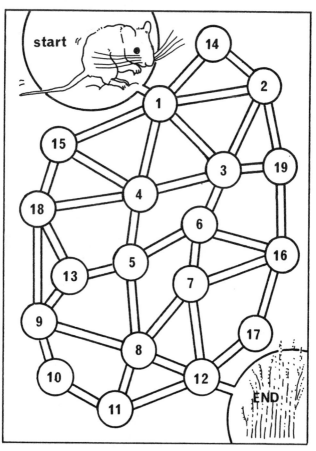

To help this dear little deer mouse reach the wheatfield, follow the number path from 1 to 12. Do not touch any other numbers.

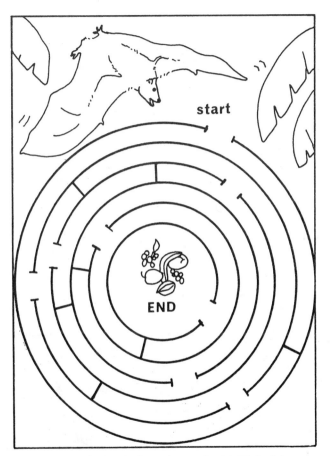

start

END

The flying fox is batty over fruit! Help him
reach the center for a rain-forest feast, and see
why he is also called a fruit bat. 37

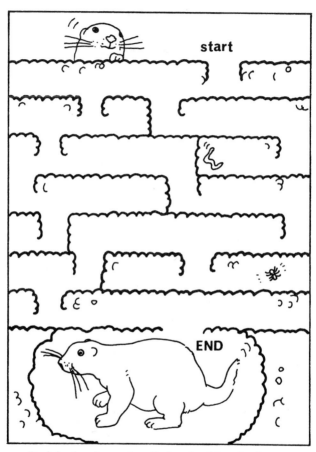

start

END

Prairie dog hears her father barking for her to join him in the family burrow. Help her find
the correct path.

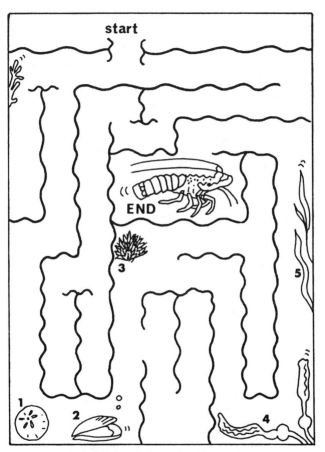

To find the spiny lobster in the sea you must pass: (1) a sand dollar; (2) a clam; (3) a sea urchin; (4) a kelp plant; and (5) seaweed.   39

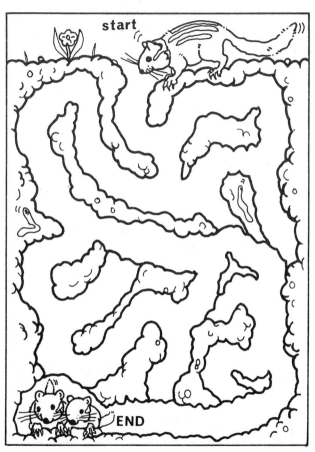

Mrs. Chipmunk's cheeks are filled with seeds for her two babies. Help her find her way to them through her underground burrow.

40

start

END

These two grasshoppers must hop through this maze to find the grain they love—but they cannot hop over any lines!

41

start

END

It is morning and these kangaroo rats must return to cool dark burrows under the desert sand. Help them find a safe place to sleep at the end!

Mom's little tadpole is growing into a frog! Find the correct path he must swim to reach his mother.

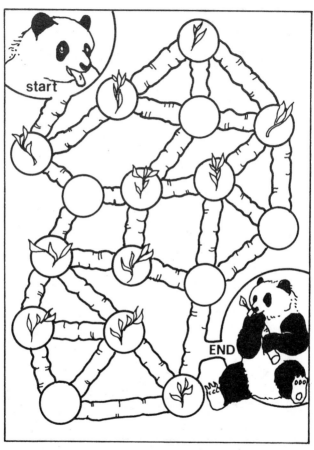

Help panda eat all the bamboo shoots on his way to his sister, without crossing any empty circles.

The tallest animal, the giraffe, spots his friend drinking and wants to join him. Help him find the way.

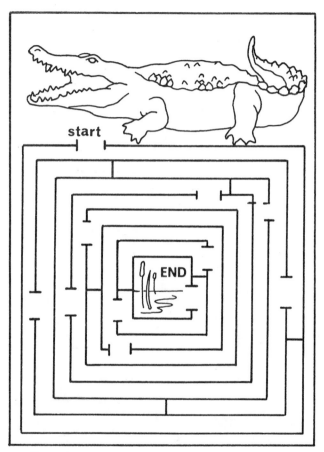

start

END

Crocodiles love to hide in swamp water to surprise prey. Find a path for this hungry croc to take to the swamp.

46

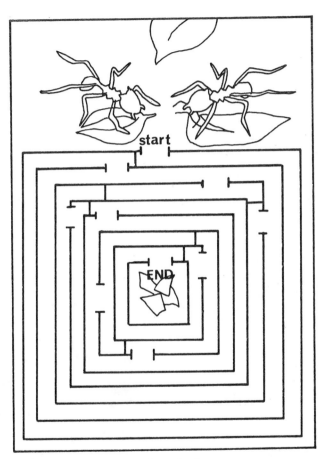

start

END

Find the path that these leaf-cutter ants must follow to bring delicious leaf pieces to their nest.

47

Solutions

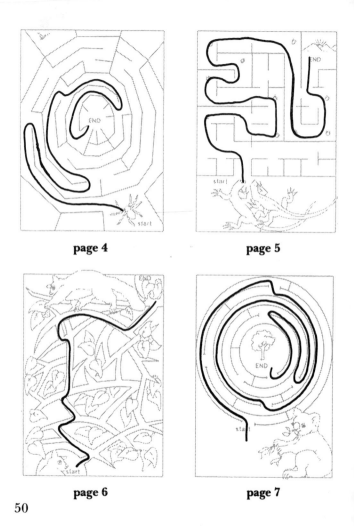

page 4

page 5

page 6

page 7

50

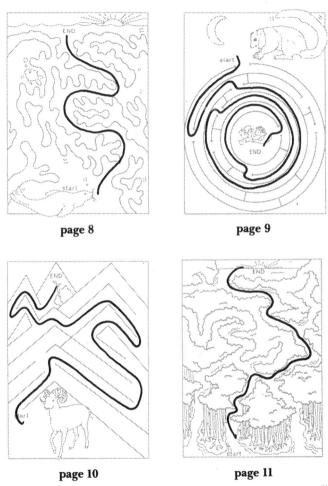

page 8

page 9

page 10

page 11

51

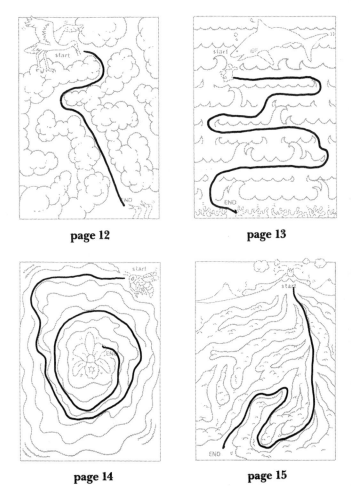

page 12

page 13

page 14

page 15

52

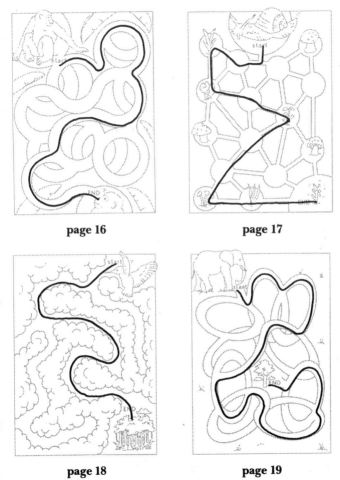

page 16

page 17

page 18

page 19

53

page 20

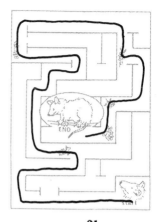

page 21

page 22

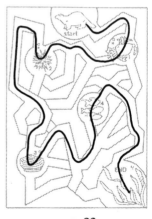

page 23

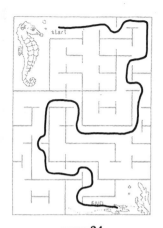

page 24

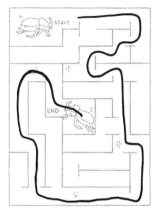

page 25

page 26

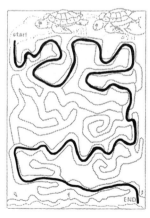

page 27

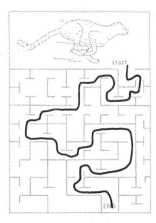

page 28

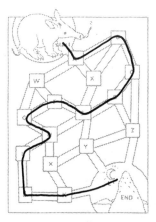

page 29

page 30

page 31

page 32

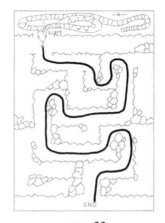

page 33

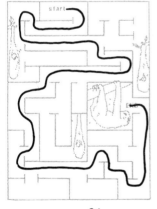

page 34

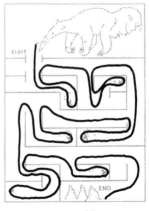

page 35

57

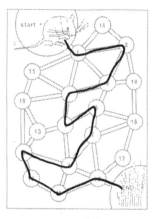

page 36

page 37

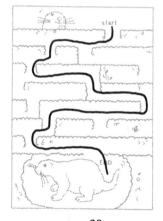

page 38

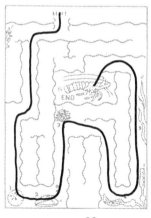

page 39

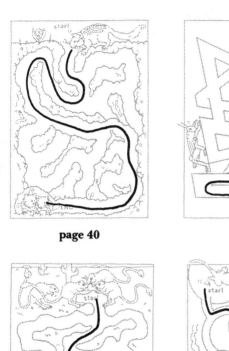

page 40

page 41

page 42

page 43

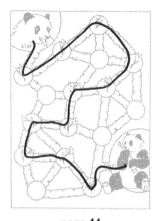

page 44

page 45

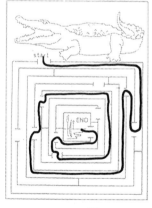

page 46

page 47